Meet Me
at Low Tide

Meet Me at Low Tide

Poems and drawings
by

Theresa Le Flem

'Meet Me at Low Tide' Anthology of poems and drawings

Published worldwide 2016 by Theresa Le Flem.

Copyright © Theresa Le Flem 2016

The author Theresa Le Flem has asserted her right under the
Copyright, Designs and Patents Act 1988
284694159

ISBN – 13: 978 – 1532793080

A CIP catalogue record for this book is available
from the British Library.

Cover illustration from an original painting
by Northamptonshire artist Royston Pittam

Cover design by Theresa Le Flem

Black & white drawings by the author
reproduced from her sketchbooks

For further information please visit the website:

www.theresaleflem.wordpress.com

For my dear husband Graham
whose wonderful support and encouragement
helped to bring this work to fruition.

Preface

Dodger encountered Oliver Twist on the road to London with the words: "I'm at low-water-mark myself - only one bob and a magpie; ..." They were both penniless. This line inspired me to write the title poem: 'Meet Me at Low Tide'. I was reminiscing about the time when I first met Graham, the wonderful man who is now my husband. Artists and poets are often more productive under pressure, but in recent years, the happiness and security I have found later in life has enabled me to write and publish three novels before embarking on this anthology of poems. Some of them go as far back as thirty or forty years. Those originally scribbled in old notebooks and on the backs of envelopes are published here as they were found.

    Surprisingly, in spite of moving house many times, these scraps of paper have survived and take their place alongside more recent additions. Similarly, the black and white drawings are reproduced from the numerous sketchbooks I have filled over the years. They are not illustrations specially drawn to suit each poem as you might expect. I have inserted them alongside poems which seemed to suit them. One advantage of being a hoarder, which I am, is that things rarely get thrown away. Brought together into a book, these items now represent a subjective account of my journey through life.

    I hope you enjoy soaking up the atmosphere of the poems written about visits to Romney Marsh in Kent. This is where, years ago, I spent many happy if melancholy summer days. The countryside and the rugged coastline of Cornwall have also been major sources of inspiration to me. Then there are more disturbing topics, as with Ireland: e.g. 'Thoughts on The Troubles' and other events in the news. 'New York after September 11th' holds a personal meaning for me since one of my sons was caught up in the tragedy. Recently I've been moved to write about the distressing sight of so many refugees seeking sanctuary. 'Migrants' is a poem which enabled me to give an immediate response to a subject which worries me.

    In this collection my feelings are laid bare on occasions. Observations, emotions, experiences, decisions – these are things which make us who we are. There are some in a lighter mood, satirical even, but many ring a sad note; it can't be helped. This after all is a testimony of my life and it hasn't all been easy. As in my novels, poems pop into my head and I often don't know where they are leading. But here they are for you, the reader, to delve into and hopefully find something in them which means something special to you. This is the joy of poetry: just a few carefully placed words can convey a feeling which would normally be – well, beyond words!

Theresa Le Flem
April 2016

CONTENTS:

A Wealth of Dreams

My small cat jumps up close
She proceeds to spin
a warm cuddly haven for us both
with her kneading paws
and pressing face
Her cold damp nose against my neck
she forms and massages a nest
of perfect sleep it seems
within to curl us both
in one safe place

My cat purrs her way towards a great sleep
pressing her body into my shoulder
me heavily into the armchair
the old cloth of it brushing against worn wallpaper
fusing me and my cat and the house into a cocoon of sleep

I would sleep too
but my thoughts in this nucleus of peace
are intensely awake
Focussed on moving pictures so alive
that I almost think my dear parents are within reach

My purring cat it seems knows more than I
about the wealth of dreams
how they tease and flicker so the soul

Oh, but I would give back my childish rebel causes
and step into the spaces left behind them
to visit once again my young predicament
of what to choose to do in life
and do it

An Olde Kentish Lament

There won't be no hop-pickers 'ere
next year and no hop-pickin' kids
to sit down 'ere and stare
to tumble an' rough-house on the hop-field edge
an' no hop-pickin' boots an' no gossip to spread

For there won't be no hop-pickin' done 'ere by hand
nor money paid out to no hop-stained crowd
It'll all be done by machinery see?
The whole field be harvested 'fore you can swear

Now they've got this machine they'll take over it all
Tear up all the hops by the roots grass an' all
torn up an' chewed over
till the field's butchered cruel

The sun an' the starlin's might find a few strewn
but the lorries'll take it an' leave the field bare
Our whole summer's work
gone in one afternoon

4

Archaeology

Traces of history in archaeology
trapped between layers
of granite quartz and slate
It doesn't preserve the how or why
only the when and where

And what was there, and no voice, no sound
no witness to declare the innocent
who now extinct lie there
Just a trace
of who they were
A clue a fragment
like a game they've set
for our amusement

A huge unfathomed sea
rose up its might one day
and came to crush and pound their fragile town to clay
Of course the ages came and ages went
and there was no encouragement
to coax the seeds of peoples' souls
from out their hiding places 'neath the soil
No-one called their names or said:
Throw up a shoot! Cast off your coverlet!
Come out!

The glaciers moved, the seas boiled
encased their world and all was silent
It left a sliver of their lives, but now
such strange mementoes trowels unearth
A gemstone shining in a buckle belt
fragments of a pot, a bone
a curious silver ornament
Their fate was cast that day, poor folk
Their lives were crushed in a closed book,
till some quiet person present day,
came patiently to pick away with trowel and time
and with a shock they thrilled to find
and shouted to their friends
'Hey Look!

At a Party

My eyes searched for your eyes
like a ship for a lighthouse
in the dark

I floundered in a crowded room
sensed no direction
Glasses chinked as laughter mimicked
my imminent disaster

I spoke and threw some lifeline of words
towards the light
which was YOU

I felt your beam search me out
encompass me in security
heave me up out of the sea
and breathe on me

You took me in your arms
and introduced me

Dear heart
You took the darkness
out of my night
the day you found me

Caphouse Colliery, Yorkshire

I stepped a hundred years into the past
in what seemed four hundred years
The cage lift dropped
into the shaft of centuries
Coal-mining in a Yorkshire pit
that paid with peoples' lives

A miner was our guide, he said:
'Close your eyes, open your eyes -
What colour do you see?'
I would've said "Black"
but the miner said: 'Look!
It's no colour at all!
Follow me!'

Down the darkest of tunnels
with a lamp, pale and damp,
'Mind your head,
watch your feet, mind the rats!'
he cried

I clung to my lamp as I followed
him down
A child of six and his mother were there
Ghosts of time lost in history,
and three children more,
all there working together
scraping coal on their knees
it had made their hands bleed
No-one saw them but me

'Fill a truck, drag the weight!
Fill it up, drag it back,
Come on you! Move yourself!'
The harsh gaffer's voice
No-one heard it but me
'Keep up!' the guide shouted.

'But the tunnel's no wider
than the poor boy's mother!'
I said, but my throat had dried

I stayed back and helped
what little I could
I was sore, almost blind
but the woman was kind,
helped me gather the coal
in the tunnel so small
that her small boy of six
was too tall

Meet Me at Low Tide

I'm at the point where clouds are touching
west wind singing, stars ascending
shallow waters, crystal waves
they call me with their night time cries
the cormorant, the herring gull
the sandpiper, the oyster-catcher
Play for me your sweet guitar
sing to me songs from afar
bring me to a softer place
hold me in your safe embrace
let me kiss your face

Meet me at low tide
at the fading of the light
where I'm wakeful and alive
when the tide is turning round
where my fingers trail in silver
in the shadows of the shallows
Lift me up out of the ocean
carry me with giant strides
up the beach to reach dry land
there we'll find nocturnal sighs
let me kiss your eyes

Meet me at low tide
when I'm at my saddest
no pennies for my purse
and no words for my novellas
Come gently now and take my hands
dry my feet with sun-warmed sand
hold the shells that I've collected
comb my hair that's so neglected
wrap me in your leather jacket
let me share your moon's eclipse
let me kiss your lips

Migrants

S hown less regard than a litter-bin
blown over in the wind they come
migrants from Syria and West Africa
all the unwanted people spill from boats
tumble and scramble in a reckless flow
of superfluous desperate humanity
As a river overflows its banks
they flood but have nowhere to go

An assortment of rags, paper and plastic
fluorescent life jackets, bottles and bags
curiously silent and mute they swarm
but their voices break cover on landing
as they shout to each other
and to those who would beat them
and shoot them, this battle of chances,
this army of want and need is driven
like a driverless train at speed
in confusion - the flesh, the children,
their bodies against fences
erupt and crumble in a rattle of steel
as a volcano flows over, they've come to take cover

Small pieces, large pieces, tents and tarpaulins
ugly coarse cotton, blankets and fleeces
woollen hoods, scarves, and poor little faces
brown eyes frozen like films on screens
with sights best forgotten, vivid and molten,
of bleeding, of bones, of cruelty, bombs
deafening decibels ringing just ringing
terror pursues them, dirty and bruised
asylum rejects them, like flotsam and jetsam
they come to beg shelter
and we say – go home?

Luxury cruises pass by rubber dinghies
turn a blind eye, they're a nuisance to tourists
Life-boats save lives but these
are anomalies, bulging with orphans,
old folk and families
near death or dying,

Refugees risking all they have known
for the waves, and the hunger, to find a new home
And the family man
who gambled their lives
for a chance to succeed
for a dream enterprise
just to live as we do, to be free and secure -
must try even harder, must try or go under!

Now he weeps
now he cries, in exhausted surrender,
as governments meet
and discuss over banquets
the outcome of war that nobody wanted
and no-one foresaw
and all they can say is: go home

Mother Nature

In the morning
she shook out and spread the fields
with a chequered tablecloth
and lay freshly baked bread from the cornfields
cream and butter churned from milk
from the cows outside her window

At lunchtime she called her family to eat
bluebells danced from the woodlands
wrens and robins flew into her arms

After supper she lit the fire
drawing the cold lambs to warm and huddle beside her
bringing the cats all purring
and wrapping her soft tweed blanket
around the shoulders of her memories

Raking out the ashes
she roasted chestnuts shaken from the sweet chestnut tree
by autumn gales
and toasted mushrooms sprung from soft mossy banks
in summer shade
She told stories from the holidays
loud as the birds' chorus

At bedtime
she shook out her patchwork coverlet
plumped up the pillows of summer's white clouds
bathed her children in the dew
and wrapped her arms around the moon

My Tears
have become Poems

My tears have become poems
that splash onto the page
Salt tears build up in caves like this
solidify like stalagmites, shine like stars
in the universe
bathe the faces of the moon
It doesn't matter year on year
if no-one's there to hear

This may sound cruel
but pain at least yields something
from out of those dark nights
to fuel the day

And in case you think I shouldn't cry
be silent as the cormorant
not give way, not write
I mean, not write the way I do
to make a point
well, it's consequential,
words fall from my eyes
as freely
as wounds bleed

So if you hear them
just dry them on your sleeve
please

My First Flight

My appetite for speed's like a raging thirst
as drums beat I leap
towards that space that we're devouring
With engine roaring strength
in every sinew Huge!
Clambering and striving to build up the pace
in this irresistible race
My longing aches
I reach forward
body buzzing with anticipation
desperation as a rush comes of acceleration
suddenly now in a surge
we're really moving!

And I with it
as a rider on a horse
faster and faster
I grasp the metal of the clasp
roaring shaking breathing breaking
whistling seizing every sinew straining
till the very speed itself outruns the course
and I surrender

At once we are at last
helplessly FAST!
Full-throttle as my dream ascends
cushions the soft belly of the aeroplane
as clouds in generous applause
make way for us
I bow to love as the plane
in an ecstasy of speed
casts the earth to miniature
and majestically
effortlessly takes flight

New York
after September 11ᵗʰ 2001

American flags hang dismally
like forgotten laundry slung across balconies
dirty and betrayed

A grey skin of steam
plumes by the Hudson River
It echoes the smoke in our memory
Something to fill the gap
Where the twin towers stood like brothers
proud against the skyline
mothers search for sons
There is no looking
only seeing
disbelieving

American flags in tatters torn
like skin like someone waving
at the moon
It's so unreachable untouchable this
enemy of life
No amount of kindness or forgiveness
seems enough

When hate itself becomes the sword
that pierces every word and thought
What can dilute the poison draught?
Who can achieve a goal in life
if death itself
is the task?

Two cylinders of buildings
where people starting work
carrying coffee, filing letters
are ignited by a spark
Death such as this
makes history itself unworthy
of the task of recording
so many lives
lost senselessly

We have this hole in Manhattan to fill
It aches
it kills us still
they all belonged to us you see
now we're loosed from it
but we don't feel free
Our question lies uncomfortably
Why not me?
Why not me?

November the Fifth

Fireworks have no enchantment in Belfast
bangers sound here as common as
song thrush birds
Between their bread, their wine
the bullets blister
and fires crackle soft as churning butter
Bonfires here have been lit before
'tis nothing new
Fear has no novelty when history is raw
Betrayal, plotting, secrecy
your Guy Fawkes lies propped up
shot dead inside his door

Children's hands wave sparklers
of the deadly kind
their fathers', brothers', grandfathers' deaths
have made them blind
No, they won't smile
at coloured showers in the sky
or pretty drops of blood
that fly from Catherine wheels

No, they won't shout with glee
nor e'er forget it
they've had their excitement
and still re-pay the debt

Of Irish Peatlands

B eloved strange land
speak to me in your mother tongue
of the bracken history crackle dry
where the faintest spark from steel-tipped boots
could set a flame to start

Where eyes shine in the ever-dark
tell me the stories that grow thick as trees
In this undercover your sisters and brothers,
bones bark and ashes compress black in ditches
and bog lands all wet sliced, like cheeses

These sticky black molasses hills
have hands that reach and catch
and trap up to the neck

Forgive me
in your mother-tongue forgive me please
Your hunger's ceased
and you, your wedges cut
stacked-up for drying in the sun
So tell me
when will all this anger, slow to burn, be over
or will it ever end?
If stones are bread and soil is fuel,
if water is wine
then wine, my friend, is blood

Oisin of Ireland

Niamh, Queen of the Land of Youth, crossed the Western Sea on a magical horse and asked the giant if his son Oisin would come with her back to live in the Land of Youth. Oisin therefore left Ireland and went with her, promising his father he would return to visit him soon. However, Oisin fell in love with Niamh during their time together. He also grew homesick. After what he thought was three years, Niamh let him borrow her magical horse so he could go home to see his father. She made him promise never to dismount or even touch Irish soil.

When Oisin arrived home he discovered his father had died years before. In sadness and confusion he was travelling back through Ireland, when he was asked by some men working by the side of the road to help them move a standing stone. Oisin reached down from the horse to help, but he fell off. Upon touching the ground he instantly became an old man. Never more would he return to the Land of Youth and his beloved queen.

O isin, how spitefully your homeland treats you
  piling years on your shoulders
  making brittle your bones
locking your vision away forever
So playfully she pains you
and imprisons you

Your homeland soil, Ireland
how she called your name from exile
how she awaited your return

Oisin, so you returned at last!
But your journey came too late
Your trek brought tears
years for hours
centuries of history unspent

You left your lovely Niamh alone
in yearning for one breath of home
But now, not pain nor blood
no road shall you now leave again

Ireland holds you fast
and though your Niamh calls you from afar
she calls, she calls eternally in vain

*Niamh pronounced 'Neev'
Oisin pronounced 'Uh-sheen'

Old Age

That time is here again
  when men become boys
  and women girls again
Who play at dressing-up and sing
and dance and care but nothing,
nothing of the real world

The boys with their trains and sticks
fight each other in a model town
of building bricks with nothing,
nothing more than bubbles tossed to kick
into their goal

That time is here too soon my friend
when memories burned
much stronger once than now
and fires fade in the eyes
of girls and boys
who were once full grown
and now are babes again

Old Country

A ah, I miss the old country
its brown grass reeds, wicker-basket
hedgerows, wild scraped heathlands
and mint trodden fern
Those old dog-leather cracked bees-waxed boots
smoke stained, tobacco plaited
auburn ended fire-tipped chestnut glowing curls,
bright flames that dance like May-pole happy girls

Aah! I remember the old days,
by bean-roasted coals we sat
and turned our tongues to song
so bewitched by summer willow switches
whisky snatches, mulled warm summer misted wine,
berry-red skies, owls calling, twigs snapping
night frosts, prodding us to keep awake

Aah! I remember home of long ago
The blacksmith's forge, the heavy scent
hot irons, black scorched steel rods glowing
horses breathing, stamping steaming
Such excitement we could never sleep
but sang instead, shared stories laughed
and talked until the embers glowed no more

Yet they glow again, look there! I see the pictures in the fire
Warming peaceful swarming summer misted evenings
Their warmth is kindling anew!
Draw your chair up close, do you not see
among the coals your childhood dreams?
Come close now close your eyes
let memories melt and settle
in the candle-wax of time

On Being Deaf

I've found a place in my mind for you
a space of silence dusted thick
with carpets wool and cloth
and spools of flax and calico
Safety in solitude

In this place women work
spinning threading winding weaving
The shuttles fly back and forth
in a dreaming
in a rhythm-like pulse
like a March-hare leaping
Weft and warp, warp and weft
the heart of all looms
back and forth back and forth
here and there
silently
safely deaf

One Girl on a Train

Girl on a train
met her blink and look away
caught her look and blink
a day beginning, stop to think
what is she doing?
Standing there half-on, half-off the train
she hesitates, the door hangs open
Would she, could she, who does she stare after
way across the platform?
Who? Where?

Empty vague, grey vacant, plain
who went I wonder then?
She turned stared, met my
gaze, abandoned then
perhaps, or caught as
shifting shuddering train-shod steps
come heavily, whistle blows, about to start
In she gets again, she falters, climbs aboard
the door slams ending her dilemma

Wildly she looks for a seat
sits like a pale animal by the window's glare
seeing nothing no-one's there

She stares
her grey moist empty eyes
have shadows left by his thumb-prints
on her lovely eyelids
Sad goodbyes

On Going to Work

I dreamt I gave my dog away
Who's fooling who? I fool myself
I gave myself away

On waking to a dawn without the joy of day
without time, I mean to own that joy
I could have died inside my bed
for giving away my day

And once during the morning's work,
when one isn't supposed to be
intensely private and alone
but Busy, Talkative and Active,
altogether Normal and OK
I found a moment of perfect silence
just hanging in the air!
No-one, it seemed, had noticed it
or felt it being there

It touched me on the shoulder
And brought tears to my eyes
What are you doing here? It asked
Where is your quiet garden now?
And where is the dog who loved you?

On the Path to St. Mary's

Y ou could hardly see her
as I climbed the path to St. Mary's
She was stooped over something
like the shadow of a boat half-hidden
But this was a churchyard solid as stone
and no water ripples on old dry bones
But there was she
a whispering frantically
fidgeting raw-fingered a knotted rope

I heard a lapwing scream
far off across the marsh as there she
now with a lamp in the evening fog
climbed into the boat and was
pushing away weakly
from the side of the church

But it was turf, not sea, the soil
solid-clogged as heavy as clung to my boots
Yet as I watched
the tiny craft dipped
keeled over and took water
Sure as I heard again that bird-like scream

she was drowning
Helplessly she went down
and slipped into the ocean field

It was a dry-land drowning
such a quiet death
on a damp stretch of grass
in the evening mist
I couldn't help her

On Parting Ways

Give me the dust grey sand
spilled from your feet from the desert
dusted sand filled shoes that spill
from your socks that sting my eyes
and taste my tongue to salt

Salt is like blood it springs to the eyes
like tears only sweeter, who told you
to empty out your shoes, the grit
between your toes like glass

Crushed, who gave you the reason for sand
to spill between your thin fingers
much as you clasp you lose?

The time is losing you to tide
spitting and frothing and crashing
like so much noise

Who gave you time to waste and spoil
and sand to wet and dust to blow
and memories to raze?

Who gave you this to waste?
The morning's peewit
on the estuary edge, tipping
and splitting the sky with so much light

It screams its name and dives
My hopes fade
as sand and waters meet
so we divide

Our Family Grave

(On discovering the Oxley family grave of my great-great-grandfather at Rolvenden, Kent in 1989.)

Two hands are joined above the place
    as if to seal a pact
    Earth and roots won't shift again
to reveal the shadow of his face

If he were mine and I had lain
him here beside the path
I would rejoice to see the soil
forever furrowed by his form
buried here, packed down and levelled
planted by the grass
his country and his body one
this land to mark his life

Two hundred years and two
world wars have raged above his bed
It comforts me to think of this:
at every dawn of every day
soft dew fell on his head

Pied-Piper: The Children of China

Festival music loud and huge found them
standing still on straw hills
The children stopped playing mechanical games
looked like ships moving on pages of mist
faces unwashed and un-kissed
But they don't know what to do
where to dance
They don't know where the sound comes from
Their ears are dazzled
and they don't remember themselves

Like seeds finding the first fall of rain
they stir and murmur
and lift themselves up out of the earth
like new sprung shoots to listen
So many dry seeds fall hither
Music springs like water in a desert oasis
Children playing hypnotically hysterically
are scolded and sent home
They'll remember when they're older
But they won't know themselves

Look how advertising posters fill the sky
standing sentry in graphic language, bold colours
Their pictures tell a foreign lie
Like jewels to the eye
glistening out of reach

These beautiful children
born to a continent who sees them not
or knows not how to see them
So our princely piper plays his tune
and the children dance with the rats
brown rats, grey rats, all to skip away
hypnotized by the sound they make
They wave flags and flowers
flowers and flags
And I wave too
and wonder why there are so many children
yet so few

Porcupines' Party

I lay me down on the landscape
It's prickly but it's cool!
In the waterfalls I freeze myself
Shivering with laughing
Shattering the icicles
Porcupines, please!

I sink my teeth into sunsets
It's risky but it's sweet!
In the afternoons I prepare a feast
Fidgeting with lemons
Fumbling with nibbles
Deliciously scrumptious!
Porcupines, please!

Prayer in February

Sweet Lady, fountain of birds
Visit me with your birdsong
Fill me with your landscape
And give me air

Dear face
fountain of smiles
pour down on me fresh spring water
revive me with your dawn chorus

Virgin of Heaven, fountain of flowers
Give fragrance to your sad sister
bring friendship to your lonely child
who searches and waits
watching for your light

Fountain of blossoms
Bear fruit for me
And bring joy to me
Dearest One!

Praying in the Garden

Praying is like watering the garden
with a watering-can not a hose
carefully selecting the needy plants
and giving the water to those

Just lately my list's getting longer
I tread through my borders with care
My delicate plants are so numerous
it's hard to remember what's where

I think hard when I'm praying but feel guilty
there's so much I could spend a whole hour
So please Lord, bless all that I care for
and give me a jolly good shower!

Refreshment Required

I could do with a poem right now
a poem with ice and lemon
a tonic to wash down the years
those dry sandy nights
those troubled waters
they get you down you know

Read me a poem cocktail
mix me a love song with tears
put the glass in my hand
and read it out loud
drink a toast
and forget all my fears

I could do with a pint, my friend
a rest and a new direction
recite me a rhyme
and forget about time
read a poem
I need a distraction

Reporting back
from the Holy land

I was offered a lift with a friend
she had just returned from the Holy Land
She went with fifty-nine pounds
(not enough she said) her well-used bible
twenty-six people and a cup of tea cost a pound
(I wished she would keep her eyes on the road!)
She had been to the Holy Land
Not a grain of sand had pierced her skin
She took the roundabout awkwardly
and talked about play-groups
and Holy Communion
How she forgot to lock her back-door when she went,
how she lost her address book
but I did get the postcard, didn't I?

49

She was fortunate
she told me, in Jerusalem
they had all stopped fighting
in time for tea

The water in the hotel
was drinkable
and the people...

She changed gear and stalled the car
The people were lovely!

Romney Marsh – the dream

I think of the afternoon
we walked together
in the solitary saucer of Romney Marsh

My lungs fill with air
at the thought of it
the green fresh ringing
bird-song space
the breathing grass
and reeds all combed
and sticked with basket-work

I see the sedge-green
moss-blushed dyke banks
stalked with bull-rush
chalked with sunlight
white glazed diamond
sugar spiked

I think of you
and of your strong warm arms
around me
and my vision shimmers
like the heat wraps
glittering jewelled meshes
veiled across my eyes
where the spirit blesses

Here, oh, here more than anywhere
is where we both will come
when the day
is dusk and done
and when our breath is one

Romney Marsh – the fields

The fields
are my bed-covers
silken sheets that barely touch
barely reach
But all around me
whiteness dazzles and glitters
from surfaces of leaves
grasses
to engravings in bark
in silver birches
fine white lines etched crystal

A transparent cobweb wispy light
in its magnification
glass on the water splinters
dives and shivers
to spill upon my bed with frosty fingers

But suddenly a vision
mystical in its celebration of light
Four white swans in perfect symmetry
travel the air above my head
soft winging, calling
reaching out to the open sea
delighting me!

Romney Marsh – the isolation

There is no-one but I
basic earth
flat total sky
background brown
glazed green razor-pointed needle grass
frizzle-fried
as horizon skimming dragonflies
wing invisibly by

Nothing but I
my breath draws in a mile of sky
breathes out a pool of vapour
blanket soft
to wrap the spider thread of thistle-crop
in dew white precious drops
even my breathing disturbs the sleep
as salt marsh frogs chirrups
resonate

I lay down with the sheep
that nibble timelessly the silent emerald quilt
remotely here perhaps a wire humming
fingertip soft waving reeds
like heaven harps wind strumming
here the woolly heads in dream-like symmetry
spread far and wide as some sweet patterned cloth all brightly
coloured green
with nothing hiding

56
56

Romney Marsh:
the memories

O that I should make a passage
back to Romney Marsh
the warblers reed to play and flight to see
where bulrush sway their heavy rods

Down by the dyke a turquoise kingfisher's sheen
is all that's seen
as a silver moment splashes into day

What time is it that sheds a tear at itself?
For in its parting, without being or becoming
any other thing than space?

It's space, life, mist
wind warm as breath on an autumn morning
Who gave this nameless directionless watery desert
its place upon a map so pierced by progress
noise and change

that by its very innocence
its gentle head is bridled

its broad back is mounted
and from the flat horizon
its spirit is lead away
to somewhere stone and grey

O that I should again make passage to the marsh
and forget as she forgets
the cutting of the knife
but breathe and speak again of silent things
see the dragonflies and weep the joy of years

with grazing sheep cropping the contours
of the earth
in patient acceptance
of the life, the outlook and the prospects
of grass

To sheep it remains after all
the spinning, continuing
timeless space
of Romney Marsh

Sleep

I need to sleep
deeper than the night can take me
sounder than my own exhaustion
will allow me

I need to bathe my inflamed mind
So sore is it with unfamiliar words
thoughts that sear my sensitivity
faces voices noises
It is all too much for me
I need to sleep

Small Death in China

In China death of one
small body is but a breath exhaled
vanished into the humid air

A tiny perfect face plump
now but soon dry
clouds that form pictures
in the sky bear witness
as they too travel back
in time from birth back
back in time towards
oblivion
unborn again
not mourned

This baby was a living
child and not a cloud
her face was like
her mother's till the gutter
dried her eyelashes to dust

She may have sighed or cried
who knows? When now
rolling like a rubber
she erases
her own brief life

An idle reader of a newspaper
rocks back on his chair
drinking coffee
while apathy turns pages

Song of a Desert Flower

The wetness of dew is my saviour
but how much longer
must I wait for rain?
I can't hold my tongue
Skies play with clouds to tease me
armfuls of black cushions toss about
One drop on my scarlet lips
to wake me
then no others

O I can't bear this dry bone bedding
give me wings!
Let me fly to find a drink
and moisture sprays and dappled showers
Where is my mother's milk
and where my honeyed seasons?
O I can't hold my tongue!

Song of Eve

Cradle me you earth
   that warms the stones of people's hearts
   cover me with your hands
     Sleep me again
as you once in me slept soundly
I in you the darkness
I in you the night
I in you the name
that calls the word of God
Reclaim me for your own
and take me home

Spaces in the Wild

I love your knotted
thistle tangled wilderness of hair
your eyes as blue as smiles up from a baby
waked at morning
I love your hands a miniature of man's
but strong pale skinned belonging to bone-ivory
dream-stained bleached white reverie

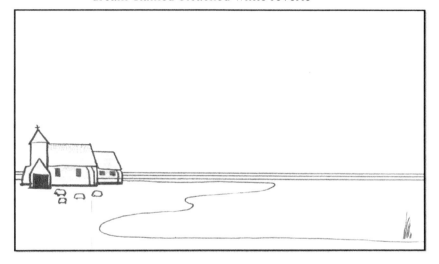

I love your heart long lost
on some strange coastal marsh
remote, some eerie place where no-one haunts
where gulls on winds embrace
those spaces open sacred wild
In salt-tanged spray
midst screams and cries
you stand unguarded conscious blind
I love you come I do
I love your lonely mind

Spirit of Place

I saw the wild stretch
sand swept abandonment
that place where you once lived
the sea has now erased
I saw the winter's waves
crash over my memories

and that funny paper-cut-out look
you gave me yesterday

Grey, those recollections soar above me
strange, they beckon me to follow on
Don't you haunt me
Don't you dare haunt me with your spirit of place

I saw the wild stretch
sand swept abandonment
that place where you once lived
the sea has now erased

Strange Marsh Visitor

She came in out of the winter night
there was rain on her shoulders
staining her hair from chestnut to raven
Thin as a willow her body looked
damp as a lamb, limp as a dead thing shed on the field

She came in and stood by the open door
blue with the cold salt wind, not speaking
her eyes overshadowed by something outside

I took her hand like a small silk mouse
feeling the weight of it grudgingly given
the fingers unmoving, the eyes of her glazed
for she came in from the marsh
where the soul is enslaved

And all these days and nights long since
though all she left was a waft of grass
though we can scarcely now recall her face
the cold of her has never left this house

Sunshine

S uddenly she came
as sunlight through crystal glass
driving solidity out of the piano
evaporating everything laughing

leaving heavy fabric furniture
vaporising

she came dividing melting
liquefying everything

clustering warm trembling colours
into her bare arms

breathing warming purring
on soft cloud carpeting
her eyes
dissolving

Sycamore Tree

L ove to live on a tree top
cradled like a kitten
in that soft deep green
curled-up like a cat
in a sycamore lap
In the oak with a head
bushy thicket fresh
holding me with sponges
in bundles of branches
with cushions to pillow me there
like marshmallow
I'd love to sleep up there
between sky-blue sheets
where no-one could find me
and where I could sleep
curled up like a cat
in a sycamore lap

Teenager's Lament

You won't catch me goin' to church
Church? It's just gone out o' fashion
Like flares an' them platform shoes
Wouldn't be seen dead goin' to church, man
it's not cool sittin' there in them pews

You won't catch me on a Sunday
kneelin' down sayin' no prayers
I'll be out there surfin' the web, man
hangin' round havin' some beers

an' the church, yeh, it's just full of old folk
they wouldn't want me walkin' in
It's so borin' it's like a museum
all they talk about's evil an' sin

Well…

Me old gran's just died, didn't know that
till I went back home 'bout eleven
they said: sit down, lad, got some bad news
old Gran, she's been taken to heaven

She liked goin' to church, my ol' gran did
never went out, only to church

She used to dress up an' sit with her friends
suppose now they've been left in the lurch

I told 'er I'd go with her one day
I would've – I meant it as well
d'you think now she's dead, like, I've 'ad it
y'know, me gran up there all sorted
an' there's me, y'know,
stuck down in hell?

The Artist

S ilence shuffles in a noiseless hush
like ballerina's slippers rubbed in chalk
Paper money counted in a quiet room
damp fingers turning pages
of a reference book while eyes blink and stare
towards the distance of receding sound
from no-one to no-where

Breath let out not in
sighs given
tennis balls roll downhill
and settle
footsteps on grass lawns
white sheets on wooden floors
blankets drying on hedges

She had come to paint a watercolour
in the garden
it was hot
rose petals settled on ledges
a strand of her hair
caught

The Beachcomber

To find a sea-sucked pebble
I would search with you
To be dazed by the waste
sight-crazed by these spat-out sweets
Jewels of dissolving sugar
who could want for more?
If you gave me a stick
to pick the teeth of the beach
we'd clatter through air
on those hills of broken china
in our minds those things we'd find there
I would come

Sea-washed fragments, buried treasure
There together rocks would rumble
boiled sweets of crystal quartz
sticky toffee stuck with tar
cockle shells and jet black mussels
scrambled in a shambles
of tangled fishing nets
and faded rubber sandals
lollipops, plastic bottles without tops
claws of spider-crabs
To find a sea-rinsed piece of glass
sky coloured rainbow fragments

discarded by the past
I would search with you
to find the pieces of my life
washed up freshly glistening anew
given up by time's long tide
to string again the beads once lost
now you are by my side

The Bride's Dress

In this village isolation they fight over love
fought over wedding-dress torn
ruined white wedding veil sweet
slight street-fight First Holy Communion night
pale cheeks stained tears pure confusion

Who upset them all, this love, this cart of love?
Who stole the child from out its mother's arms?
Who hurt the babe and made the woman cry?
What drove the men to stop the women sewing,
piled hurt upon hurt to rage against that dress
and tear its white from white pure innocence?

Who tore the precious cloth? Who stripped the bride?
Who, in heartfelt hate, through fear demands perfection?
This family, who came then to the priest
in simple sore frustration
were born again in marriage
Blessed by anger's ceasing
in their Christian forgiving
The daughter dressed in white
Married her love that night
their banquets wedding feasting
seemed suddenly alright

The bridegroom was uncomfortable
his shirt too tight his shaven face too sore
but he had seen enough and swallowed
all he knew before
She came up to the alter in her virginal bliss
in her calm amnesia of faith
carried reassurance
and love pure love
and innocence
was shining from her face

The Calling

Can you hear my piper play? Can you see
    that one so strange?

Paper ships move in the mist
Faces unwashed and un-kissed
I don't know which way to turn

Seeds finding the first spring rain,
reaching out to drink again
Desert oasis a playground,
children scolded and sent home
I look back over my shoulder

Who are you?
with the name I can't remember
playing your tune, you hypnotize
all of our lives

Lead me away with you
and let me see where the sound comes from
what your music will show me
when we reach the mountain valley
together

The Candle

I love your candle flame of flesh
as you wiggle your hips
in the darkness mesh
I love your blade song-tickling tongue
licking wax-white lids
of eyes that see beyond dreams
to where our fears kiss

I love your warmth
the way you give your body to the heat
and wrap
and shawl-soft wrap yourself
out of the cold

The Coin

We stepped into another world
as we entered the dark steel cage
a hard hat, a coin, a heavy belt
and a miner's lamp to hold
'Get cosy!' called the collier
as nineteen of us packed in
He clanged the metal door closed
shutting out the sun

'Don't use yer lamp till yer needs it, he said, 'It don't last long.'
Three hundred feet the lift dropped down
the steep shaft shone as wet and black as jet
it swallowed us, that pre-historic throat
monstrous in its treatment of honest working folk

Shuddering it shrank our breath
stopped with a lurch and eyes white
he signalled our reverse into a pitch dark dungeon,
void of air, sheered with wooden plank and pillar
'Follow me' the collier said.
'Turn on yer lamps an' don't be scared.'

He waved we stumbled, lamps so feeble shadows cast
he told of dynamite and dust and lives all lost
and old ghosts voices mumbled as we trod upon the grit
I could have crawled for safety's sake
as passageways gave way to caves
afraid my lamp would fade

We stopped by a cavern, a small steel door
a boy he said would've pitched just there
to wait for his mother's cart of coal
lit by his candle, bought with his own poor wage

He'd watch and tend the flame and measure how the time
would slip and drip the wax
lest the darkness snuffed it out and made him blind

Back out of history we came, visitors from another time
We left behind the stories and the dank black hoards
of treasured coals, the bounty hauled
the wealth of gold, the weight of rocks
we left it thankful to be up and breathe the cool spring air

The collier gravely took the lamp, the belt, the hard hat,
then the coin
'We count yer down an' count yer back –
or not,' he said, 'sometimes.'

The Condor

Above a lost dominion
he takes off like a plane across the desert sun
outsider in a world outside of everyone
In burning ice flamingos dive
and flowers thrive in fields of fire

On wings of death he travels up
the condor stretches out
across the universe
a predator to challenge
even life itself
On melting stones
a seagull rests
and fountains play
in warm desire

Into the scarlet morning sky
from mountain canyon
diamond quartz and rubies shine
to catch the light inside the vulture's thirsty eye
A humming-bird collecting wine
a butterfly
fanning flames of terror

The Days of Gypsy Gold

In the days of gypsy gold my friend
In the days of gypsy gold
down the days of dock and dandelion
to pick the sloes they'd roam
Bright fires would glow like fireflies
through the trees they placed each foot
so cautious not to snap a twig
startle the prey to bolt away
and escape the cooking pot

In the days of gypsy gold my friend
In the days of gypsy gold

They were skilled enough to catch a few
the rabbits, they were often fooled
Carefully creep an' set the trap
run to hide and bide your time
so's to fill the cooking pot
they would fill their stomachs yet

In the days of gypsy gold my friend
In the days of gypsy gold

Tattin' an' potato pickin'
hop-pickin' an' fruit pickin'
could turn their hand to anythin'
to earn a few old bob
Then they'd roam down meadows strewn
with mushrooms, cobnuts, chestnuts, apples
rich an' plenty can't deny
they were the best
the days of gold
the days of gypsy gold

The Drawing

Black bone of the leaf
embedded deep inside the paper
over, taught-stretched,
comes the smooth green skin
Over the skin the grey green pith
that pounds the seed into the dry page
from the pith comes the silt
and the silver light frothing
like winged moths

Through the white of the leaf
you see her
crouched up inside the skin
huddled, tight-fisted,
eyes closed, body twisted
up inside the fabric of the leaf
Beneath the surface hidden
her face a secret from the air
Yet you see the pencil move now
to reveal her

The Famine

In silhouette against the African sun
they rise as one people, flock together
Suddenly inexplicably they all turn
turn automatically westward
like a flock of birds turn
as one
as at the report of a gun
They turn away from despair
like a herd of starved submissive creatures
They turn away and look into the sun

Their freedom is spent now
lost in hunger months ago
They seek nothing and move without seeing
human beings but little more
than remnants of cloth
dusty bones travelling the desert floor

Those once strong Ethiopian men
stand derelict
wistfully suspended in time

And their beautiful women
their once beautiful women
bathe their dreams in imaginary moisture
of milk and oil
in preparation for the eve of their dying

Mothers who gaze silently
into their children's eyes
see the flames of hope still flicker

It's only hope that lives on
hope and love
that never dies in Africa

The Felling

Intense cold perhaps
  brought the blade into being
  forged by the contrast
after summer, it came
like a rainbow thrown off course
to reap and slice at the quiet ash
that had served each season
undisturbed
our timepiece
and our kitchen window's shade

Such cruelty must have ground
that blade, sharpened it on a
whetstone, held it ready
for the felling
I saw it
bite into the green wood
and drink the white fibrous
sponge of the body-sap
till the full grown tree went down

The men stopped then, to roll a
cigarette in the fresh March air
they gazed about at their work
breathing satisfaction
and their smoke filtered out
to fill the space
where the quiet ash
had spread its firm black buds
like sooty fingertips
turned upwards

The Final Time

Somehow the day didn't get off to a start
I was still drinking coffee at ten
with newspapers spread on the settee among the pyjamas
I was just feeling the energy to begin
when suddenly it became the middle of the day
old Gran had died the final time

The first time was when her husband died
When he went, his worn cloth chair by the fire remained
even the musk of his rich tobacco pipe
lived on to capture the evening drawing into night
Alone by the cluttered table of tea-stained cups
biscuit-tin remnants of distant childhood
she used to whisper and mutter to her husband's empty chair
and sigh and close her eyes

I remember the shadow of the cat long since dead by the fireplace
a black cat whose mechanism purred its way
into their timeless existence
I remember the old railway
where the tracks gave way to gorse grass and thistle

I remember the clock that ticked in a slow damp step
through the hollows of the upstairs bedrooms
where she in carpet slippers shuffled
bringing with her from down below
the fragrance of milk and boiled potatoes

Over tea and biscuits in that worn familiar room
Granny would so often in the afternoon light
nudge me with a twinkle in her eye
just happy at home with her simple things
She had faith in herself you see,
she had a strength of will

But they came
and persuaded her out of her house,
They made her leave her old back room
And Grandad's empty chair, the fireplace bare
and her old stone sink chipped and dry
She died again there on the step I'm sure,
as she turned to go
leaving her life locked in behind that heavy door

What made her agree to leave?
To please them all perhaps
But anyway she went
To live in a modern apartment
No longer did she wash
in her old aluminium tub
on the kitchen floor by the stone sink
boiling kettles on the hob
with the gas oven lit for warmth
She bathed in a shiny bathroom
bright with steel and taps

It changed her, washed her whole life away
So far was she then
from her husband's sunburnt vegetable-dry skin
from his evening eyes and his stories
when he'd come home tired from the allotment
carrying a basket of fresh dug potatoes
for her to cook in their old fish kettle

Just before she died the final time
she walked back to her old home
breathing heavily, pale, determined
Her cottage beckoned as she drew near
though a Sold sign pierced her rose bed
and a car had crushed the lawn

She went to the back door as usual
shuffled in and sat down among them all
smiled at each of them in turn
strangers silent staring dumb
She gave a long contented sigh
'This is my house you see,' she said

The Fossil

I have another dream
which is neither yours nor mine,
it goes beyond a memory
to a time beneath the soil
to a fossil
in a rock as yet not fractured
formed but waiting
an embryonic creature!

Who says it's there, who knows
who created it and why?
Born only to be known that it had died
discovered under an apricot sky
with plumes of colours, prisms,
where the mountains gave up oceans
and spilled themselves
down, down to surround and drown
this small unnamed creature as it ran -
boiled, burned, cast into an image of itself
by its own mould

I have a fearful dream
when that from which I run outruns me
my space, my body in the space I make
surrounds me
and traps me like an insect trapped in amber
and that which I most fear imprisons
and solidifies my soul forever

The House Remains the Same

The house remains the same
in its day-time state
always day-time
for her man is out at work

Even in the early morning
before he leaves
he has already left
his packed lunch already taken
This she tells herself
contented in her way
that her man is working

The house remains the same
during the day
The woman about her washing and sewing
her face in the steamed-up mirror
seems the same
as she waits for when
his day of work is finished
when he comes home, tired
to a hot meal
and a doze by the ageing fire

But when its time
for the man to go upstairs to bed
why, he is already up the stairs asleep
and she just clearing away her things
before she too
with fresh-washed face
eyes shining
mounts the stair
half-listening for his breathing

The Magpie's Warning

Black angular magpie
white-tipped against a white chalk field
where the living plough
churns the dead soil back into its own bed

Rise up magpie rise up now
before it's too late, rise up
in the warmth of this wind
and catch your breath
before you fall like dust forever
into the dryness

Strange growing land this
It has no moisture not a
drop of green in its whole pale landscape
Brown and greyness fathoms deep
right up to where the sky meets

It's a scar of land I curse it
with my eyes sore and yet
it draws me, absorbs me in its plainness
in its desert-cup

The white-from-white black magpie flies
its parched throat raucous crow-like calls
"Beware" I'm sure it cries, "Beware!"
Don't let the flint-stones fool you
when they glitter and when the wind drags up
the dust in clouds of spray, and the sun sets
purple-pink and sits itself just right
against a silhouette
to make you say –
ah, look and catch your breath..

Beware! For all these things
experience has seen and planted in this field
and it will come the turn of someone soon
to dig this clay down deep
and claim it for his own

The Miner

Rusted iron is the way of it
and fool's gold
barren heathlands
where the trees are felled
The miner's private passions spent
on his final cigarette
before lowering his lids on the daylight
as underground he went

Maybe it was a dream inside his head
that all the ore that's smelted
beaten poured and moulded
was gold as it was red
But down to earth he went
Down to earth he went

Would he that died could rise again!
His mother prayed he would
From out of that black pit a grave
should serve him better yet

He downed the day
and moved ten tonnes
before his face appeared again
His mother caught her breath

His eyes were white as stars at night
and gold as they were red
His mother looked, his mother cried
as every night the women, wives
wait for the stars
the gold
the lives

The Music of Strangers

You have the notes inside your head
why don't you close the book and come to bed
Let me hear your music
Let me feel you play your music for me
Let me hear you, hear you, let me hear you

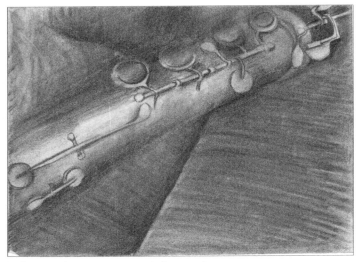

It doesn't hurt to cry at night you know
The sound of tears is music, softly flow
your kisses fall in patterns casting shadows in my love for you
Let me hear you, hear you, let me in

Play your fingers on the strands of my hair
let me 'neath your skin to see what's there
sing the melody of touching
reach out to me with sounds
caress me, I'm listening, Let me in
let me hear you, hear you
let me hear you

The Sound of My Life

I wondered what that sound was
but it was the sound of my life
rushing past my ears and out into the night

If, when you come to visit me
I'm already dead
you won't blame me will you
or call me names

just because my watercolour's wilted
and my hand's unsteady
when I paint the sky

The sky that is an open window
how I long for it to open wide
and set me free
and close again shut tight
once I have flown away

The Stranger

You show your life to me in photographs
I can't help seeing the ghost inside your eyes
It shines out from the page
and finds me searching your pale face
for why you really came
and who you really are

There are places in my life I like to hide in
but in yours they're deep as stars in space
A fragment of the darkness
tears itself away to shade your hair
and glint like some strange precious stone
your eyes

The Teacher's Baby

No blame on the child, safe in his sweet cocoon
feeding in her arms, half-forgotten,
while his mother gazes into lost reminiscences
her past loves

Oh, these were not lovers but children!
How she had loved them all!
Shabby and thin from the street
How she had gathered them to her
in her busy paper coloured classroom
skinny spoon-fed little urchin kids
who clustered in maternal bliss

How her instincts yearned towards them
and they were all born and born and born again to her
as though they were her own
and she would take them home
But this babe of hers, this half-forgotten infant,
this innocent thief! How restlessly he lies in her arms now
how restless now he cries Demanding and commanding her
to lay regrets aside and be his mother

The Tide That Changes Worlds

After the ship the Sea Empress went aground
and sank in February 1996
The Sea Empress was carrying oil to the Texaco Oil Refinery in Pembroke when
she ran aground mid-channel on rocks at St. Anne's Head. Spilling 72,000 tons of
oil into the sea, it polluted Pembrokeshire Coast National Park, one of Europe's
most sensitive and important marine conservation areas. The disaster was the third
largest oil-spillage in British history.

It could be blood except its black
it bleeds from the shadowed spectre of a ship
the wound in its hull gives oil
down into the sea with slow tireless weakness
till every bird's feather's glued

They don't mix, oil and water so they say
but when they do, God knows
an alchemy of death is done
The webbed feet curl like old dead leaves
The dead beaks burn
The rainbow colours stolen from the sky run
in crazy whirlpools of lustred lead
not pretty, not even really coloured anymore

Seals' mouths fill with molten rubber
whose fault's this? The very rocks cry out!
God knows, it must be someone's fault
these lives are not so different to our own

Screaming when we could be singing
Sinking when we should be flying
The tide that changes worlds
Change me too! Change me too!
O tide that changes worlds,
change me too!

The Tsunami

On Boxing Day 2004 a massive earthquake and tsunami occurred in the Indian Ocean resulting in the deaths of 300,000 people.

The day the sea spilled over the land
Beth's children were playing in the sand
She saw the wave and began to run
trying to gather them into her arms
And Po the ice-cream maker's stall
with sweets, candy and nuts to sell
crumpled as though it was made of sand
The day the sea spilled over the land

The day the sea spilled over the land
A wedding in the church was planned
Sumi had put on her wedding gown
and all the guests were in the town
The tables were laid out in the sun
families laughing and having fun
till the huge wave caught them unawares
and dragged them out to distant shores

The day the sea spilled over the land
dawned fine and sunny with little wind
Women at home were beginning their chores
with their children playing out of doors
Many of their fathers were fishermen
already bringing the first catch in
When the mountain of water stopped the sun
and took their lives, nearly all of them

The day the sea spilled over the land
was a day no-one ever could imagine
Like a water-colour left out in a storm
within minutes all the picture was gone
Like a sand-castle crumbling into the waves
thousands upon thousands lost their lives
We hold our breath now in shock and wonder
for fragile as a cobweb, we are torn asunder

The Working Boy

He's outside again
wanting to be where his father is
wanting to do what his father does
smoking, embracing the unbreathable air
facing the unworkable fear

He's pacing the pavement
thinking he ought to be there
working where his father works
but his age alone tempts him
to leave the job
and go elsewhere

Time

H istory,
how sad it is
when you think how
each one person tries

lifts the pen and writes
and lays the pen down
and dies

and with each lifting
a century weighs it
and within each word
a lifetime's spent

Thirst for a Glimpse of Flowers

I thirst for a glimpse of flowers
  for fresh growing things, for grass
  a prisoner in a concrete block must feel like this
A drop of pure rainwater on the step
is like a jewel dropped, a petal
precious as a baby's hand is kept

I thirst for natural things
the fragrance of burning wood
for leaves, for salt-marsh spray, for the sea
Someone to connect with me
Love would be like a cup of water to my lips
but I have no lover

Those Old Friends

Such a sad afternoon
making polite conversation
smiling
trying to be relaxed
knowing all the time
our days are counted
and we don't know how to say it

Leaving those dear friends behind
looking about you to take it in
this room, this chair
this dog by the fire
for the last time
we talk, hug
we laugh, stare

Such a cold sunny day
recounting all the times we spent together
making light of something precious
feeling hurt inside but
smiling the way you have to
just to make it easy when you say it
when you say goodbye

Thoughts on 'The Troubles'

All the time Ireland rocked
freshness washed stark
as a raft on an open ocean

We murmured together
not to each other
but to the vastness out of our hands
What alchemy of faith and hope is this?

Gentle flowers pressed
between news events
Reactionary stalks
stuck upright in marsh wastelands
Shot guns like bull-rush stems

There are other dead
not yet died but leapt
within reach, panting
praying for it
as if
death is some achievement

And why?
As birds fly from brush
their intentions leap in song
to leave the shores where
wrecked hopes lie
and venture forth with armaments
of steel and guns and cruel zeal

Brave men who braver yet would die
for Ireland
Our boys
who might on bullets speed fly home

let them live
if not to love, then why?

Thoughts on Winter

There's still snow up on the high ridge of the farm
and where the shade has kept it
stacked up grey and ugly
solid by the road
for pedestrians to stumble over
and crows to pick over

Already the rest of us have forgotten it
the birds of us singing
and those who are bulbs now bulging with life
But then those who stop to think
pause now half-way along that road
and say: Is this all us people do?
Go to work and work and go home unnoticed
day after solid day
the snow is after all forgotten
I begin to think, am I too?

Suppose I too have failed to melt
and my soft white beauty's gone
Surely as snow I am stuck here
wedged grey, frozen as sludge

half-way along the road, lost
unable even to reach my home
I mean if the warmth in you
neglects to shine on me
where will my white beauty be,
and who will remember me?

War in Ireland

Ireland
tearing yourself apart
raising dead harvests out of the soil
And all we ask is why?
On local battlefields your farmers toil
though the grain for their children's meals is spilled and spoiled
year on year

Dawn on the landscape
hears the raw voice of command
across the marsh
as through the fields fresh-ploughed
bullets fly like sprinkled seeds
fall to the fertile flesh of the land
to sow crops of colours
we all come to the market-place
to cheer for and die for
and weary our way home for
And all we ask is why?
What for? Orange scars to green
and green the harvest bleeds

Love in the hearth ever warming
yet anger in the fire ever kindling

Waiting

You sowed your orange seed
deep in the heart of my soul
for our tree, our tree of love to grow
and our sweet blossom to flower

The sun shone down on my orange grove
birds they flocked from all around
on wings the colour of flames
with their song of gentle laughter

But the seasons passed and you never came
though our tree grew tall and strong
The years passed by, you never came
though my fruit shone bright as the sun
And I'm waiting for you still
waiting for you still

Waking Early

I wake early in the morning
picking up the threads of my thoughts
from the day before
Thinking I might do more
today, and my imagined ability
to achieve, heightens my appetite for everything
even for chores that so often bore me
suddenly I can do them all!
Washing, cleaning, baking cakes,
I have all day, just watch me!

But even then in the half-light
my addiction drowsy in its vision
comes into focus
My writing beckons
with a hastening pulse
Ideas! Phrases! Pictures! Voices!
till all else replaces that domestic impulse!

I wake early, almost dawn
Disregard the chores and yawn
step into another's shoes
and see a sudden twist of plot
A furtive smile, an unlocked door
a gunshot, a forgotten coat!

Before I know it
ideas grow like a cuckoo chick
pushing all the nestlings out
demanding food demanding more
an all-consuming appetite!

The resolutions made
the night before of what I should prioritize
vanish the way of a blackbird's flight
frantic in her insect search

to feed the monster in her heart
As at first light she wakes
I too into the dawn give wing
as any anxious mother flies
to feed the darling of her eyes

I take up my pen
and write
while she does sing

Wedding Ring

I'm cold shut in
her fourth finger warmed me
till today when tears dripped
soap slipped gold rolled
me away, away from her

Hands pale fingernails torn
hurts pain as sharp as thorns
hearts dulled and cannot shine
nor sing

My time has come to speak
Her wedding ring lies in her jewellery drawer
I'm cold shut in
and she won't glow to gold again,
my bride in her wedded bliss,
nor sing
She won't warmly make my reasons rhyme
for she had much to take

She's cold, poor bride
but fine and free
Remember this: I'm just
gold jewellery in dust
not all is lost
Her youth her innocence and love
rang true when she did wear me

When You Look at Me

When you look at me
I feel like an upturned boat
I feel grief
As if seeing your face
on a departing train

Your closeness moves me almost to tears
but my awareness of you
draws me away from you

Your sweet emotional
strangely unconscious chatter
touches me
wraps me in a warm shawl

But suddenly
I feel loneliness

like a tired off-shore swimmer
like an actor forgetting his part

Winter Without Sleep

Who will rescue them?
my thoughts are hostage
in a winter's sleep
stirring fretful in a fever deep
of dreams more wakeful than myself

My Lord's love is a quiet love
he keeps presence in my soul
He doesn't speak
I'm hurting as if my mind's locked
my mouth's snaffled like a mare
my head's held fast, my words unborn

Would be a fiery day if once I spoke aloud
my anger 'gainst the injustice that's been made

I'm hurt so deep within my soul
that I can't heal can't cry or fight
I am a victim of long ago
and something's wrong that must be right

Writer's Distraction

Why is there so much distraction
to stop what I want to achieve?
I'm determined to finish that chapter
but the washing I just can't leave
I'll fill the machine but before I do
there's the cat I need to feed
And the dog needs a walk
So I put on her lead
then the phone rings…
A friend who needs to talk
talks on and on without a why or please

But while I'm in the kitchen
I pause to take an aspirin
I feel chilled, I'm about to sneeze
I haven't got time for chattering!

I get away and feed the cat
while the dog whines so I let her out
Empty the bin, put a new bin-liner in

then the timer goes off
I'd forgotten the cake!
Oh, for goodness sake!

It's cooked, it's done
take it out of the oven
an' I leave it to cool
Get the dog back in
clip her lead back on,
take my coat off the hook
open the door, grab my phone
There's a bleep and I look...

It's my neighbour next-door
She's about to call round
I don't want to offend
I say 'great!'
I say 'fine!'
and I find myself lying!
'I've just put the kettle on,
you're just in time!

A note from Theresa Le Flem, the author:

I hope you have enjoyed reading my poems and looking at the various drawings. I've been writing poems all my life. Only once did they see the light of day when I read them aloud to students while studying Art. Since then they have been tucked away in drawers. I rarely looked at them once they were written. I had two short stories published in magazines before embarking on my lifetime's ambition – to write a novel. This opportunity only came to me later in life but I now have three novels published:

The Sea Inside His Head: (Published by Robert Hale Ltd. 2012)

It is 1984, and the Kent coalfields face closure. Striking miner Bradley is haunted by the pit which killed his father. When his wife's vigorous campaigning for the saving of the pit intensifies, he retreats into his allotment to contemplate a heart-rending decision. With his sister pregnant and scared of the world discovering her secret, Bradley is faced with a difficult decision: voluntary redundancy would bring enough to buy a small-holding in the country where there is a promise of a new life for his family, but to qualify he must break the strike and defy everything his wife stands for. Dare he become a scab and risk losing the woman he loves?

The Forgiving Sand: (Published by Robert Hale Ltd. 2013)

1994, Cornwall. With the fishing industry in crisis it is becoming increasingly difficult to make ends meet in a small, coastal town. Christina's quiet beach cafe is losing money and her ruthless brother-in-law, Rene, is determined to close it down. Disabled since childhood, Christina is determined to maintain her family business but neither her mother nor her sister are interested in helping her. But when John Madison, a widowed and lonely local skipper, desperately seeks Christina's help with his young daughter she is both disturbed by him and drawn to him. Who can save her beloved Sea Cafe? And when John asks her to take a risk, will her heart be torn in two?

The Gypsy's Son: (Self-Published 2015)

Set in Cornwall in the 1950s, this moving novel explores family relationships, romance and memories. When a frightened young boy runs away from home, Gideon Tremayne, a Romany gypsy, resolves to take him back. But their journey takes a lifetime. This is a thought provoking book which delves into the past and challenges the reader to re-evaluate the meaning of life, home and survival. It's a novel about reconciliation in which the search for love and security beckons…

I occasionally give talks and attend book-signings. I am a member of the Romantic Novelists' Association, the Society of Authors and the Poetry Society. With three grown-up children and five grand-children all living abroad, I live in the Midlands, U.K. with my husband Graham and our retired greyhound. In my spare time I enjoy painting, playing folk-music on the fiddle and gardening.

If you would like more information about me and my work, please visit my website. I am always keen to hear from you, my reader, and welcome any comments you may have. Thank you

www.theresaleflem.wordpress.com

Printed in Great Britain
by Amazon

83479097R00081